AAT

Professional Diploma Synoptic Assessment

Pocket Notes

These Pocket Notes support study for the following AAT qualifications:
AAT Professional Diploma in Accounting – Level 4
AAT Level 4 Diploma in Business Skills
AAT Professional Diploma in Accounting at SCQF Level 8

British library cataloguing-in-publication data

A catalogue record for this book is available from the British Library.

Published by:
Kaplan Publishing UK
Unit 2 The Business Centre
Molly Millars Lane
Wokingham
Berkshire
RG41 2QZ

ISBN 978-1-78740-830-2

© Kaplan Financial Limited, 2020

Printed and bound in Great Britain.

This Product includes content from the International Ethics Standards Board for Accountants (IESBA), published by the International Federation of Accountants (IFAC) in 2015 and is used with permission of IFAC.

Contents

Preface

These Pocket Notes contain the key things that you need to know for the exam, presented in a unique visual way that makes revision easy and effective.

Written by experienced lecturers and authors, these Pocket Notes break down content into manageable chunks to maximise your concentration.

Quality and accuracy are of the utmost importance to us so if you spot an error in any of our products, please send an email to mykaplanreporting@kaplan.com with full details, or follow the link to the feedback form in MyKaplan.

Our Quality Co-ordinator will work with our technical team to verify the error and take action to ensure it is corrected in future editions.

A guide to the assessment

The assessment

Four units within the Professional Diploma in Accounting are mandatory. Of these, three are assessed individually in end of unit assessments, but this qualification also includes a synoptic assessment, sat towards the end of the qualification, which draws on and assesses knowledge and understanding from all four mandatory units.

Examination

Professional Diploma Synoptic Assessment is assessed by means of a computer based assessment. The CBA will last for 3 hours.

In any one assessment, students may not be assessed on all content, or on the full depth or breadth of a piece of content. The content assessed may change over time to ensure validity of assessment, but all assessment criteria will be tested over time.

Learning outcomes & weighting

Assessment objective	Weighting
A01 Demonstrate an understanding of the roles and responsibilities of the accounting function within an organisation and examine ways of preventing and detecting fraud and systemic weaknesses.	20%
A02 Evaluate budgetary reporting; its effectiveness in controlling and improving organisational performance	15%
A03 Evaluate an organisation's accounting control systems and procedures	15%
A04 Analyse an organisation's decision making and control using management accounting tools.	15%
A05 Analyse an organisation's decision making and control using ratio analysis.	20%
A06 Analyse the internal controls of an organisation and make recommendations	15%
Total	**100%**

Pass mark

To pass a unit assessment, students need to achieve a mark of 70% or more.

This unit contributes 35% of the total amount required for the Professional Diploma in Accounting qualification.

1

The accounting function

- Introduction.
- The accounting function.
- Relationships with other departments.
- Coordination between accounting and other business functions.
- Regulations affecting the accounting function.
- Understanding systems.

Introduction

Organisations and the need for control

Definition
'Organisations are social arrangements for the controlled performance of collective goals'.

Control mechanisms

Methods of control
Organisational structure
Target setting and budgeting
Direct supervision
Culture
Self-control
Control Systems – e.g. actual v budget
Control processes – e.g. control account reconciliations

Organisational Structure

How to discuss structure
The division of responsibility
The degree of decentralisation
The length of the scalar chain
The size of the span of control
Whether organisations are 'tall' or 'flat'

The accounting function

The role of the accounting function

There are four components to the function

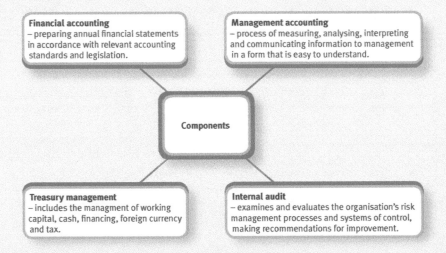

Financial accounting
– preparing annual financial statements in accordance with relevant accounting standards and legislation.

Management accounting
– process of measuring, analysing, interpreting and communicating information to management in a form that is easy to understand.

Components

Treasury management
– includes the managment of working capital, cash, financing, foreign currency and tax.

Internal audit
– examines and evaluates the organisation's risk management processes and systems of control, making recommendations for improvement.

Relationships with other departments

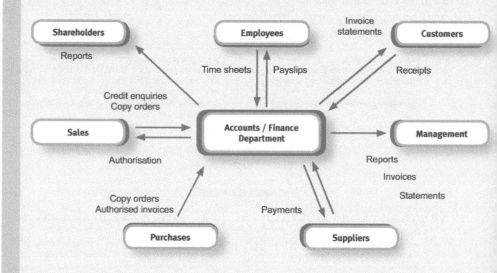

Coordination between accounting and other business functions

Department	Areas of interaction
Purchasing	Establishing credit terms Monitoring payments Inventory and cost control
Production	Cost measurements and overhead allocation Budgeting (e.g. units, quantity) Achieving efficiency and economy
HR	Recruitment and training expenditure Salary payment, estimating PAYE liabilities Reward plans, tax-efficient benefits packages
IT	Systems design and development Improving access to information Incorporating new technology into operations
Customer services	Pricing additional services (e.g. maintenance) Assessing costs of product failures Qualitative feedback on operations
Marketing	Advertising budgets Product pricing Estimating market share

Regulations affecting the accounting function

Responsibility to regulatory authorities:

- Companies House (e.g. submission of financial statement for inspection by interested parties).
- Tax authorities (e.g. HMRC for VAT, PAYE, corporation tax).
- Financial services (e.g. stock exchange for listed companies).
- Regulators, where appropriate (e.g. Charities Commission, Ofcom).

Companies Act 1985 sets out that financial statements have to give a "true and fair view".

IFRS Foundation supervises the development of international standards and guidance. It's a parent entity of:

- International Accounting Standards Board (IASB): aims to develop a single set of quality, understandable and enforceable accounting standards.
- FRS Interpretation Committee (IFRS IC): reviews widespread accounting issues and provides guidance.
- IFRS Advisory Council (IFRS AC): consults the users of financial information and offers advice to the IFRS Foundation.

Understanding systems

General systems

The environment

Inputs → **Transportataion process** → Outputs

Boundary

Example – If we are concentrating on the finance system, then sales, production and purchasing become part of the environment, and within the system boundary will be found smaller subsystems such as product costing, financial accounting and treasury.

Control systems

- **Standard** – is what the system is aiming for.
- **Sensor** (or detector) – measures the output of the system.
- **Comparator** – compares the information from the standard and the sensor.
- **Effector** (or activator) – initiates the control action.
- **Feedback** – is the information that is taken from the system output and used to adjust the system.

2

The use of key financial reports

- Financial accounting and financial statements.
- Management accounting and management reports.
- User groups.

Financial accounting and financial statements

Purpose of financial statements

The statement of financial position	Provides information on the financial position of a business (its assets and liabilities at a point in time).
The statement of profit or loss	Provides information on the performance of a business (the profit or loss which results from trading over a period of time).
The statement of other comprehensive income	Shows income and expenses that are not recognised in profit or loss.
The statement of changes in equity	Provides information about how the equity of the company has changed over the period.
The statement of cash flow	Provides information on the financial adaptability of a business (the movement of cash into and out of the business over a period of time).

Stewardship

Stewardship is the accountability of management for the resources entrusted to it by the owners or the Government.

Management accounting and management reports

Needs of management

Planning	Planning involves establishing the objectives of an organisation and formulating relevant strategies that can be used to achieve those objectives.
Decision making	In most situations, decision making involves making a choice between two or more alternatives.
Control	Output from operations is measured and reported ('fed back') to management, and actual results are compared against the plan in control reports.
	Managers take corrective action where appropriate, especially in the case of exceptionally bad or good performance.

Key reports

- Budget reports, detailing budgetary plans for future periods
- Variance reports comparing actual and budget performance, to facilitate effective control
- Reports of key performance indicators to ensure that management focus on what is important to the success of the organisation.
- One-off reports that look at individual decisions.

Evaluating a management report – factors to consider

- The basis of preparation
- The methods used
- The figures used
- The impact on people concerned

User groups

Needs of users

Investors	Need to be able to assess the ability of a business to pay dividends and manage resources.
Management	Need information with which to assess performance, take decisions, plan, and control the business.
Employees and their unions	Need information to help them negotiate pay and benefits.
Customers	Need to be assured that their supply will continue into the future.
Suppliers	Need to be assured that they will continue to get paid and on time and the financial statements will help with this.
Lenders, such as banks	Interested in the ability of the business to pay interest and repay loans.
HM Revenue and Customs	Uses financial statements as the basis for tax assessments.
The public (especially pressure groups)	Will look at the financial reports and statements to aid their understanding of profits an organisation may be making from activities to which the pressure group are opposed.

3

Internal controls

- Internal control.
- Typical control activities (SPAM SOAP).
- Internal audit.
- The purchases cycle.
- The sales cycle.
- Payroll.
- Cash and cheques.
- Segregation of duties revisited.

Internal control

Internal control consists of the following components (ISA 315):

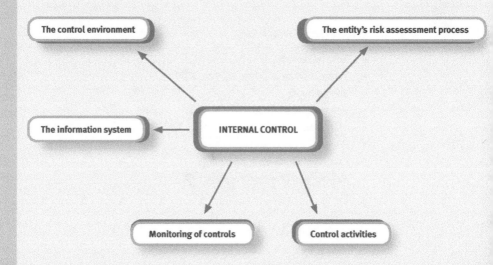

Typical control activities (SPAM SOAP)

Segregation of duties	Keep separate the custodial function, the authorisation function, the recording function and the execution function.
Physical controls	Access to assets and records is only permitted to authorised personnel.
Authorisation and approval	All transactions require authorisation or approval by a responsible person.
Management	Controls exercised by the management outside the day-to-day routine of the system.
Supervision	Supervisory procedures by the management.
Organisation	A well-defined organisational structure showing how responsibility and authority are delegated.
Arithmetical and accounting	E.g. control accounts, cross totals, reconciliations and sequential controls over documents.
Personnel	Well-motivated, competent personnel who possess the necessary integrity for their tasks.

Internal audit

Definition

'an independent, objective assurance and consulting activity designed to add value and improve an organisation's operations.'

What do internal auditors do?

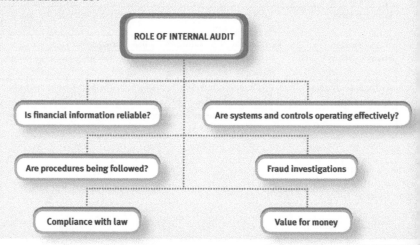

The purchases cycle

Stage 1 — Order placed

Stage 2 — Goods received

Stage 3 — Invoice received

Stage 4 — Transactions recorded in books

Stage 5 — Cash payments

Purchase system

The objectives of controls in the purchase system are to ensure that:

- all purchases are of the appropriate quality and price
- only necessary goods/services are procured
- all purchases and related payables are recorded
- expenditure is recorded in the period to which it relates
- expenditure is recorded accurately and related payables are recorded at an appropriate value.

The sales cycle

Stage 1	Order received
Stage 2	Goods despatched
Stage 3	Invoice sent
Stage 4	Transactions recorded in books
Stage 5	Cash received

Sales system

The objectives of controls in the sales system are to ensure that:

- goods are only supplied to customers who pay promptly and in full
- orders are despatched promptly and in full to the correct customer
- only valid sales are recorded
- all sales and related receivables are recorded
- revenue is recorded in the period to which it relates
- sales are recorded accurately and related receivables are recorded at an appropriate value.

Payroll

Stage 1	Clock cards submitted and input
Stage 2	Gross pay, deductions and net pay calculated
Stage 3	Other amendements input
Stage 4	Final payroll calculated and payslips produced
Stage 5	Payments to employees and tax authorities
Stage 6	Payroll costs and payments recorded

Payroll system

The objectives of controls in the payroll system are to ensure that:

- only genuine employees are paid
- employees are only paid for work done
- employees are paid at the correct rates of pay
- gross pay is calculated and recorded accurately
- net pay is calculated and recorded accurately; and
- correct amounts owed are recorded and paid to the taxation authorities.

Cash and cheques

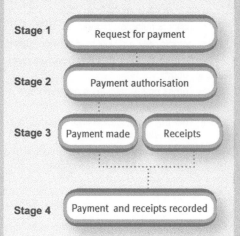

Stage 1 Request for payment

Stage 2 Payment authorisation

Stage 3 Payment made | Receipts

Stage 4 Payment and receipts recorded

Cash cycle

The objectives of controls in the cash cycle are to ensure that:

- petty cash levels are kept to a minimum, preventing theft
- payments can only be made for legitimate business expenditure
- cash and chequebooks are safeguarded
- receipts are banked on a timely basis
- cash movements are recorded on a timely basis.

Segregation of duties revisited

Purchases	The persons who raise purchase orders should be independent of the ledger keeping function, the stock recording and control subsystem and the cheque.
Sales	The persons responsible for preparation of sales orders should be independent of credit control, custody of stock and recording sales transactions.
	The credit controller should be independent of the sales order clerks.
	The warehouse/despatch department should be independent of sales order preparation, credit control and invoicing.
	Sales invoicing should be independent of sales order preparation, credit control, warehouse and despatch departments.
	The sales ledger clerk should be independent of sales order preparation, credit control, warehouse, despatch and sales invoicing.
	The sales ledger control account should be maintained independent of the sales ledger clerk.
Cash	The persons who sign the cheques should be different from those who handle the authorisation of purchase invoices.
	The persons who are responsible for opening the post, preparing the paying-in details and controlling the sales ledger should be separate functionaries.

4

Internal controls in computerised systems

- Information systems controls.
- Data security.
- Integrity controls.
- Controls.
- Systems integrity in a network environment.
- Contingency controls.

Information systems controls

General controls

General controls relate to the environment within which computer-based systems are developed, maintained and operated and are generally applicable to all the applications running on the system.

Personnel recruitment policies	To ensure honesty and competence.
Segregation of duties	To minimise tampering with programs or data.
Proper **training** programmes	To ensure competence and reduce errors.
Physical security of hardware and software	To prevent accidental or malicious damage or natural disasters.
Authorisation procedures for program amendments and testing	To prevent unwanted changes being made.
Back-up procedures (maintaining copies of files off-site, back-up facilities).	To ensure data and systems can be recovered.
Access controls.	e.g. firewalls and anti-virus checkers.
Hacking prevention measures	To ensure the system is not accessed during data transmission (hacking).
Efficiency measures	Controls to ensure that the computing resources are used efficiently.

KAPLAN PUBLISHING

Data security

Data security measures involve different aspects:

- **Physical security**, such as the security of data storage facilities, from flood as well as unauthorised access
- **Software security**, such as maintaining a log of all failed access requests, and
- **Operational security**, with regard to such things as work data being taken home by employees, and periodic data protection audits of the computer systems.

Physical Security controls

Fire systems and procedures	e.g. fire alarms, heat and smoke detectors.
Location of hardware	e.g. away from risk of flooding.
Regular building maintenance	e.g. attention to roofs, windows and doors will reduce the risk of water penetration and make forcible entry more difficult.
Physical access controls	e.g. security guards to check identification and authorisation, CCTV, using badge readers or coded locks on access doors from public areas and electronic tagging of hardware.

Individual staff controls

Logical access system	e.g. identification of the user, authentication of user identity and checks on user authority.
Personal identification	e.g. PIN, fingerprint recognition, eye retina 'prints' and voice 'prints'.
Storage of CDs, removable data storage devices in secure locations	e.g. back-up data is stored in a fire-proof environment on-site, and occasionally some form of master back-up is removed from the installation site completely.

Integrity controls

Activities

Data integrity means completeness and accuracy of data. For decisions to be made consistently throughout the organisation, it is necessary for the system to contain controls over the input, processing and output of data to maintain its integrity.

Input activities	File processing activities	Output activities
• data collection and preparation • data authorisation • data conversion (if appropriate) • data transmission • data correction • corrected data re-input	• data validation and edit • data manipulation, sorting/ merging • master file updating	• output control and reconciliation with predetermined data • information distribution

Controls

Input Controls	Validation and processing controls	Output controls
Verification	**Validation**	**Batch control totals**
• Verification	• Comparison of totals	• Batch control totals
• Type checks	• Comparison of data sets	• Start or report / page number / end of report markers
• Non-existence checks	• Sequence numbers	• Distribution lists
• Consistency checks	• Range checks	
• Duplication checks	• Format checks	
• Range checks	**Processing**	
• Input comparisons	• Standardisation	
• Batch and hash totals	• Batch control	
• One-for-one checks	• Double processing	

Systems integrity in a network environment

Risks

- Hardware/software disruption or malfunction
- Computer viruses
- Unauthorised access to the system

Controls

- Physical access controls
- User identification
- Data and program access authorisation
- Program integrity controls
- Database integrity controls
- Anti-virus software
- Surveillance
- Communication lines safeguards
- Encryption
- Firewalls

Contingency controls

Disasters

In computing terms, a disaster might mean the loss or unavailability of some of the computer systems.

Contingency Plan

- Standby procedures – so that essential operations can be performed while normal services are disrupted.
- Recovery procedures – to return to normal working once the breakdown is fixed.
- Management policies – to ensure that the plan is implemented.

- **Controls**
- Distributed support, where computing is spread over several sites.
- Reciprocal agreement with another company.
- A commercial computer bureau.
- Empty rooms / equipped rooms.
- Relocatable computer centres.

5

Ratio analysis

- Ratio calculations.
- Interpreting ratios.
- Interpreting financial information.
- Limitations of ratio analysis.
- Linking ratios and control problems.

Ratio calculations

Profitability	Liquidity	Gearing	Investor
• ROCE • Gross profit • Operating profit • Asset turnover	• Current ratio • Quick ratio • Inventories days • Receivables days • Payables days	• Gearing • Interest cover	• EPS • Dividend yield • Dividend cover • P/E ratio

Profitability

$$\text{ROCE} = \frac{\text{PBIT}}{\text{Capital Employed (Equity + Debt)}} \times 100\%$$

$$\text{Gross profit margin} = \frac{\text{Gross profit}}{\text{Revenue}} \times 100\%$$

$$\text{Operating profit margin} = \frac{\text{PBIT}}{\text{Revenue}} \times 100\%$$

$$\text{Asset turnover} = \frac{\text{Revenue}}{\text{Capital Employed}} \times 100\%$$

Short-term liquidity

$$\text{Current ratio} = \frac{\text{Current Assets}}{\text{Current liabilities}} : 1$$

$$\text{Quick ratio} = \frac{\text{Current Assets} - \text{Inventory}}{\text{Current liabilities}}$$

Efficiency ratios (working capital)

$$\text{Inventory days} = \frac{\text{Inventories}}{\text{COS}} \times 365 \text{ days}$$

Trade receivables collection

$$\text{period} = \frac{\text{Trade receivables}}{\text{Revenue}} \times 365 \text{ days}$$

Trade payables collection

$$\text{period} = \frac{\text{Trade payables}}{\text{Purchases (or COS)}} \times 365 \text{ days}$$

Long-term solvency

$$\text{Gearing} = \frac{\text{Debt}}{\text{Equity}} \times 100\% \text{ or } \frac{\text{Debt}}{\text{Debt} + \text{Equity}}$$

$$\text{Interest cover} = \frac{\text{Profit before interest and tax}}{\text{Interest}}$$

Investor ratios

$$\text{EPS} = \frac{\text{Earnings}}{\text{Shares}}$$

$$\text{Dividend yield} = \frac{\text{Dividend per share}}{\text{MV per share}} \times 100\%$$

$$\text{Dividend cover} = \frac{\text{PAT}}{\text{Dividend}}$$

$$\text{P/E ratio} = \frac{\text{Price per share}}{\text{Earnings per share}}$$

Interpreting ratios

It is important to understand the meaning of the ratios as well as calculating them for the exam.

Interpreting financial information

Introduction

Financial statements on their own are of limited use. In this chapter we will consider how to interpret them and gain additional useful information from them.

Users of financial statements

When interpreting financial statements it is important to ascertain who are the users of accounts and what information they need:

- shareholders and potential investors – primarily concerned with receiving an adequate return on their investment, but it must at least provide security and liquidity
- suppliers and lenders – concerned with the security of their debt or loan
- management – concerned with the trend and level of profits, since this is the main measure of their success.

Commenting on ratios

Ratios are of limited use on their own, thus, the following points should serve as a useful checklist if you need to analyse the data and comment on it:

- What does the ratio literally mean?
- What does a change in the ratio mean?
- What is the norm?
- What are the limitations of the ratio?

Limitations of ratio analysis

- Ratios do not provide answers; they merely highlight significant features or trends in the financial statements. They usually highlight areas that need further investigation.

- Be mindful of seasonal trade as accounting year-ends are often just after the seasonal trend is over when the business is at its best.

- Watch out for window dressing in the financial statements such as collecting receivables just before the year-end in order to show a larger cash balance and lower receivables than is normal.

- Accounting ratios are based on accounting information and are only as accurate as that underlying accounting information.

- If comparisons are to be made they must be with companies with a similar trade, otherwise the pattern of ratios will be different and the comparisons meaningless.

Linking ratios and control problems

From problems to ratios – examples

Control issue	Impact on financial statements	Key ratios affected
Fraud where items are stolen from the warehouse	• Cost of sales will higher than expected	• Fall in gross and net margins
Credit controller ill	• Receivables balance will be higher than expected	• Receivables days higher • Quick and current ratios higher
Theft of cash	• Less cash than expected	• Quick and current ratios lower
Fraud where items are sold to a friend at a very low price	• Sales lower than expected • Gross profit lower than expected	• Fall in gross and net margins • Receivables days lower

From ratios to problems – examples

Ratio	Basic causes	Possible control issues
Gross margin down	• Prices lower and / or costs of sales higher	• Sales managers giving excessive discounts • Theft of inventory • Excessive waste / obsolescence of stock • Cut-off problems • Price rises from suppliers unchecked due to purchase orders not being authorised correctly
Inventory days higher	• Excessive period – end inventory • Cost of sales lower	• Purchased too much inventory due to purchase orders not being checked properly • Purchase invoices mis-recorded • Errors with time sheets

6

Fraud

- What is fraud?
- Fraud risk management.
- Fraud detection.
- Fraud response.

What is fraud?

Definitions

- Dishonestly obtaining an advantage, avoiding an obligation or causing a loss to another party.
- Note: distinction made between fraud and errors (unintentional mistakes).

Examples of fraud

Crimes against customers	e.g. pyramid schemes; selling counterfeit goods
Employee fraud against employers	e.g. falsifying expense claims
Crimes against investors, consumers and employees	e.g. falsifying financial statements
Crimes against financial institutions	e.g. fraudulent insurance claims
Crimes against government	e.g. social security benefit claims fraud; tax evasion
Crimes by professional criminals	e.g. money laundering
E-crime by people using computers	e.g. spamming; copyright crimes; hacking

Fraud risk management

Prerequisites for fraud

- An ability to rationalise the fraudulent action and hence act with dishonesty.
- A perceived opportunity to commit fraud.
- A motive, incentive or pressure to commit fraud.

Fraud prevention

- Anti-fraud culture
- Risk awareness
- Whistleblowing
- Sound internal control systems

Fraud deterrence

Only when potential fraudsters believe fraud will be detected and when whistle-blowers believe they will be protected will there be an effective deterrence of fraud.

Fraud detection

- Performing regular checks.
- Warning signals/fraud risk indicators.
- Failures in internal control procedures
    - Lack of information provided to auditors
    - Unusual behaviour by individual staff members
    - Accounting difficulties.
- Whistleblowers.

Fraud response

- Response plan:
    - Internal disciplinary action
    - Civil litigation
    - Criminal prosecution
    - Responsibilities clearly set out

7

Improving the accounting system

- Reasons for change.
- Justification of change.
- Implementing changes – dealing with resistance.
- Implementing changes – approaches.

Reasons for change

Reason for change	Example
Regulation changes	VAT rules change
Growth	Old manual approach cannot cope with growth
New information flow	The government could introduce new report requirements
Short-term capacity issues	PC failure
Identified weakness	e.g. need to introduce new levels of authorisation
Changes in the environment	Increased focus on environmental factors
New products	Switch to ABC

Justification of change

Cost-benefit analysis

Tangible costs	Intangible costs
• One-off costs (e.g. development, buying new equipment) • On-going costs (e.g. maintenance, replaceable items)	• Staff dissatisfaction if systems are poorly specified or implemented. • The cost of increased staff mistakes and reduced performance during the learning period after a new system is implemented. • Opportunity costs. • Lock-in costs. Purchasing a particular solution can bind a company to a particular supplier, reducing its ability to take advantage of future developments from other providers.
Tangible benefits	**Intangible benefits**
• Savings in staff salaries, maintenance costs and consumables. • Greater efficiency. • Business benefits gained through improved management information. • Gaining competitive advantage.	• More informed or quicker decision-making. • Improved customer service, resulting in increased customer satisfaction. • Freedom from routine decisions and activities, resulting in more time being available for strategic planning and innovation. • Better understanding of customer needs through improved analysis of data.

Techniques

• Payback • NPV • SWOT

Implementing changes – dealing with resistance

Resistance

Job Factors	These generally revolve around fear – fear of new technology, fear of change or fear of demotion or levels of pay.
Social Factors	The people affected may dislike the potential new social dynamic (or like the existing social scene and not want that to change).
Personal factors	These, by definition, are more varied as each person may react differently to a particular change.

Response

Source of resistance	Possible response
• The need for security and the familiar.	• Provide information and encouragement, invite involvement.
• Having the opinion that no change is needed.	• Clarify the purpose of the change and how it will be made.
• Trying to protect vested interests.	• Demonstrate the problem or the opportunity that makes changes desirable.
• Dislike the social upheaval.	• Organise social team building events.

Implementing changes – approaches

Testing

Realistic data testing	The new system is tested against normal transactions to ensure it operates as expected.
Contrived testing	The new system is presented with unusual data to see how it reacts e.g. negative sales invoices.
Volume testing	A common problem with systems is that they fail to cope when volumes increase, so this is tested in advance. Systems may crash or slow down excessively.
User acceptance testing	Systems are often designed by IT experts but then used by people with much less IT skill.

Changeover method

Direct	The old system ceases and the new system takes over on the same day.
Parallel	In this system both the old and new systems are run at the same time.
Pilot	The new system is piloted in a particular location. In this way operational bugs can be identified and removed before wider implementation takes place.
Phased	This is similar to a pilot, but it is the phrase used when the system is introduced in stages or in one sub system at a time.

8

Ethics and sustainability

- Ethics.
- Fundamental principles.
- Examples.
- Sustainability.
- Benefits of acting sustainably.
- Sustainability and the accounting system.

Ethics

What is ethics?

- Morality – the difference between right and wrong – 'doing the right thing'.
- How one should act in a certain situation.

Why should we bother with ethics?

Pros	Cons
• To protect the public interest	• Increased cost of sourcing materials from ethical sources
• To avoid discipline/fines	• Lose profit by not trading with unethical customers/suppliers
• Improved reputation	• Waste of management time?
• Good ethics can attract customers	
• Good ethics can result in a more effective workforce	
• Ethics can give cost savings	
• Ethics can reduce risk	

Fundamental principles

Confidentiality	Information obtained in a business relationship is not to be disclosed to third parties without specific authority being given to do so, unless there is a legal or professional reason to do so.
Objectivity	Business or professional judgement is not compromised because of bias or conflict of interest.
Integrity	This implies fair dealing and truthfulness.
Professional Competence and Due Care	The necessary professional knowledge and skills required to carry out work should be present.
Professional Behaviour	All relevant laws and regulations must be complied with and any actions that would bring the profession into disrepute avoided.

Examples

Accounting issues	Creative accounting.
	Directors' pay.
	Bribes.
	Insider trading.
Production	Should the company produce certain products at all, e.g. tobacco.
	Should the company be concerned about the effects on the environment of its production processes?
	Should the company test its products on animals?
Sales / marketing	Price fixing and anticompetitive behaviour.
	Is it ethical to target advertising at children?
	Should products be advertised by junk mail or spam email?
Personnel	Discrimination.
	The contract of employment must offer a fair balance of power between employee and employer.
	The workplace must be a safe and healthy place to operate in.

Sustainability

What do we mean by 'sustainability'?

* Sustainable development is development that meets the needs of the **present** without compromising the ability of **future** generations to meet their own needs.

(The UN's Bruntland Report).

* A sustainable business is a business that offers products and services that fulfil society's needs while placing an equal emphasis on **people**, **planet** and **profits**.

(The Sustainable Business Network)

Examples of unsustainable practices

Economic

* Underpayment of taxes – not contributing to maintaining the country's infrastructure (schools, roads, etc.).
* Bribery and corruption.

Social

* Rich companies exploiting third world labour as cheap manufacturing.

Environmental

* Long term damage to the environment from carbon dioxide and other greenhouse gases.

Benefits of acting sustainably

- Potential cost savings – e.g. due to lower energy usage.
- Avoiding fines – e.g. for pollution.
- Short term gain in sales – e.g. if customers are influenced by sustainability related labels on products.
- Long term gain in sales – e.g. due to enhanced PR and reputation.
- Better risk management – e.g. pre-empting changes in regulations.
- Sustainability is one aspects of a firm's commitment to CSR.

Sustainability and the accounting system

The Accountancy Department

- The paperless office – how much of the paper used in the accounting department is justified?
- Emailing invoices to customers rather than posting paper versions.
- Emailing statements to customers rather than posting paper versions. .
- The energy usage for lights, the machines and for heating.
- The use of sustainable materials for the office furniture.
- The level of carbon dioxide produced (if any).

'What gets measured gets done'

- The accountancy function can help champion sustainability by suggesting environmental performance measures and measuring these KPIs.

9

Recap of key aspects of Financial Statements of Limited Companies

- IFRS foundation.
- Legal framework.
- IASB framework.
- IAS 1 Presentation of Financial Statements.
- The fundamental principles of the AAT Code of Professional Ethics.
- The threats.
- Safeguards.
- Uses of ratios.
- Key ratios.
- Limitations of ratio analysis.

IFRS foundation

The structure of the International Financial Reporting Standards Foundation (IFRS Foundation) and its subsidiary bodies is shown below:

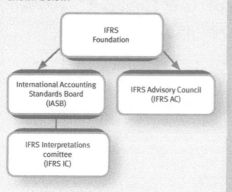

Key Point

- The IFRS Foundation is an independent not for profit foundation based in the US whose trustees appoint the members of the IASB, IFRS AC and IFRS IC.

- The IASB is responsible for developing and issuing new accounting standards. The IASB issues International Financial Reporting Standards (IFRSs) and has adopted the previous International Accounting Standards (IASs).

- The IFRS AC advises the IASB on priorities in its work and informs the IASB of the implications of proposed standards for users and preparers of financial statements.

- The IFRS IC draws up interpretations if a new problem arises or gives guidance on the application of a standard where unsatisfactory interpretations exist.

Legal framework

- In the UK, companies must prepare their financial statements following the rules laid out in the Companies Act 2006 (CA06).

- The CA06 has been amended to reflect the fact that some companies prepare their financial statements based upon the application of IFRSs.

- In the UK, the Financial Reporting Council (FRC) prepares accounting standards. In recent years there has been a process of harmonisation between UK and International standards and the majority of UK standards are now equivalent to IFRSs.

IASB framework

The IASB's Conceptual Framework for Financial Reporting identifies the principles on which accounting standards are to be developed. It aims to assist in the preparation of financial statements, development of new standards and to reduce alternative accounting treatments.

Key Point

- The underlying assumption of financial statements is that they are prepared on a going concern basis.
- There are two fundamental qualitative characteristics together with four enhancing characteristics:

The two fundamental qualitative characteristics:

- **Relevance** – financial information is regarded as relevant if it capable of influencing the decision of users.

- **Faithful representation** – this means that financial information must be complete, neutral and free from error.

The four enhancing qualititative characteristics:

- **Comparability** – it should be possible to compare an entity over time and with similar information about other entities.

- **Verifiability** – if information can be verified (e.g. through an audit) this provides assurance to the users that it is both credible and reliable.

- **Timeliness** – information should be provided to users within a timescale suitable for their decision making purposes.

- **Understandability** – information should be understandable to those that might want to review and use it. This can be facilitated through appropriate classification, characterisation and presentation of information.

Elements of the financial statements

Asset: a resource controlled by an entity as a result of past events and from which future economic benefits are expected to flow to the entity.

Liability: a present obligation of the entity arising from past events, the settlement of which is expected to result in an outflow from the enterprise of resources embodying economic benefits.

Equity: the residual interest in the assets of the entity after deducting all its liabilities.

Income: income consists of both revenue and gains. Revenue arises from a business's ordinary activities such as the sale of goods. Gains represent increases in economic benefits such as a gain on disposal of a non-current asset and are not normally shown within revenue.

Expenses: expenses are losses as well as expenses that arise in the normal course of business such as cost of sales, wages and depreciation. Losses represent a decrease in economic benefits such as losses on disposal of non-current assets or disasters such as fire or flood and are often shown separately in the financial statements.

Recognition of items in the financial statements

Recognition of (i.e. recording) an item in the financial statements occurs if:

- the item meets the definition of an element
- it is probable that any future economic benefit associated with the item will flow to or from the entity
- it can be measured at a monetary amount with sufficient reliability.

IAS 1 Presentation of Financial Statements

IAS 1 provides formats for the statement of profit or loss, statement of financial position and statement of changes in equity as well as setting out six accounting concepts that should be applied:

- **going concern** – the business will continue in operation for the foreseeable future

- **accruals** – the effects of transactions and other events are recognised as they occur and not as cash or its equivalent is received or paid

- **consistency of presentation** – items in the financial statements are presented and classified in the same way from one period to the next unless there is a change in the operations of the business or a new standard requires a change in presentation

- **materiality and aggregation** – each material class of similar items shall be presented separately in the financial statements

- **offsetting** – assets and liabilities and income and expenses cannot be offset unless a standard requires it

- **comparative information** – should be shown for all amounts reported in the financial statements.

Accounting policies should be selected so that the financial statements comply with all international standards and interpretations.

An entity must make an explicit statement in the notes to the financial statements that they comply with IFRS.

The fundamental principles of the AAT Code of Professional Ethics

Outlined below are the key principles of the AAT Code of Professional Ethics.

Professional competence and due care

A professional accountant has a continuing duty to maintain professional knowledge and skill at the level required to ensure that a client or employer receives competent professional service based on current developments in practice, legislation and techniques.

Objectivity

A professional accountant should not allow bias, conflict of interest or undue influence of others to override professional or business judgements.

Confidentiality

A professional accountant should respect the confidentiality of information acquired as a result of professional and business relationships and should not disclose any such information to third parties without proper and specific authority unless there is a legal or professional right or duty to disclose.

Professional behaviour

A person should not act in any way that is unprofessional or does not comply with relevant laws and regulations.

Integrity

A person should be straightforward and honest in performing professional work and in all business relationships.

The threats

The following are all examples of behaviour that could threaten an accountant's objectivity or independence from their clients:

The self-interest threat – may occur because of a financial or other interest held by the accountant or a family member.

The advocacy threat – may occur when an accountant is asked to promote or represent their client in some way. In this situation the accountant would have to be biased in favour of the client and therefore cannot be objective.

The self-review threat – when work you have previously prepared needs review – you cannot audit your own work.

The familiarity or trust threat – this occurs when the accountant is too sympathetic or trusting of the client because of a close relationship with them.

The intimidation threat – may occur when an accountant may be deterred from acting objectively by threats – actual or perceived.

Safeguards

Safeguards are controls to reduce or eliminate threats. They fall into two broad categories:

(i) Safeguards created by the profession, legislation or regulation. Examples of these include:

- Educational, training and experience requirements for entry into the profession.
- Continuing professional development requirements.
- Corporate governance regulations.
- Professional standards.

- External review by a legally
  empowered third party of the
  reports, returns, communications
  or information produced by a
  professional accountant.

(ii) Safeguards in the work environment.
Examples of these include:

- Policies and procedures to
  implement and monitor quality
  control of engagements.

- A disciplinary procedure to promote
  compliance with policies and
  procedures.

- Policies and procedures to monitor
  and, if necessary, manage the
  reliance on revenue received from a
  single client.

Uses of ratios

Key Point

- Ratio analysis is a means of interpreting financial statements.

- Users will review the financial statements and make decisions based on the information given. Ratios are calculated and compared with:

  - the performance of the business in previous years

  - the budgeted or planned performance in the current year

  - the performance of similar businesses.

- Ratios can assist in pointing the user of the financial statements to areas where the company may be performing particularly well or badly. They do not in themselves provide an answer but they can help in indicating the right direction for further investigation.

- The types of ratio to use will depend on the user of the information. For example, banks and lenders will be interested in liquidity ratios; management will be interested in profitability ratios.

- Ratios fall into several categories:

  - profitability ratios

  - liquidity and working capital ratios

  - investor ratios.

Key ratios

Ratios are important tools to assist in the interpretation of financial statements. You must learn these ratios and be able to calculate and interpret them as an exam task will require you to do both.

Profitability ratios

- **Return on capital employed (ROCE) =**

$$\frac{\text{Profit from operations}}{\text{Total equity + Non-current liabilities}} \times 100$$

ROCE is very important as it shows the profit generated from the capital employed in the business. If ROCE has increased it is due to either increases in profitability and/or increases in asset utilisation.

- **Return on shareholder's funds =**

$$\frac{\text{Profit after tax}}{\text{Total equity}} \times 100$$

- **Gross profit percentage =**

$$\frac{\text{Gross profit}}{\text{Revenue}} \times 100$$

This shows the profit made on revenue before accounting for overhead costs. An increase or decrease may be due to a change in the sales mix, changes in costs or selling prices.

- **Expense/Revenue percentage**

$$\frac{\text{Specified expense}}{\text{Revenue}} \times 100$$

- This can apply to any expense

- **Operating profit percentage =**

$$\frac{\text{Profit from operations}}{\text{Revenue}} \times 100$$

  This shows the profitability after taking into account expenses. A change may be due to changes in costs. You might expect an increase if sales have increased, but must watch out for costs that are rising above any sales increase as it may be that costs are not being controlled.

Liquidity

- **The current ratio =**

$$\frac{\text{Current assets}}{\text{Current liabilities}}$$

- **The quick ratio =**

$$\frac{\text{Current assets} - \text{inventory}}{\text{Current liabilities}}$$

These two ratios show whether a business can cover its current liabilities from current assets. The quick ratio removes inventory as this is the least liquid current asset. If the ratio is too low, it may suggest the business will have trouble paying current liabilities and if the ratio is too high it may suggest that working capital is not being used efficiently.

This ratio can vary greatly from industry to industry.

Use of resources

- **Inventory turnover =**

$$\frac{\text{Cost of sales}}{\text{Inventories}}$$

- Companies have to strike a balance between being able to satisfy customers' requirements from inventory and the cost of having too much capital tied up in inventory.

- **Inventory holding period =**

$$\frac{\text{Inventories}}{\text{Cost of sales}} \times 365 \text{ days}$$

This shows how long inventory is being held before use.

- **Asset turnover (net assets) =**

$$\frac{\text{Revenue}}{\text{Total assets - current liabilities}}$$

- **Trade receivables collection period =**

$$\frac{\text{Trade receivables}}{\text{Revenue}} \times 365 \text{ days}$$

If the receivables collection period becomes too high, the business may suffer from poor cash flow. Retail companies do not usually have receivables so this ratio would be irrelevant for those companies.

- **Trade payables payment period =**

$$\frac{\text{Trade payables}}{\text{Cost of sales}} \times 365 \text{ days}$$

Extending the payables payment period can be a cheap source of finance but companies run the risk of upsetting suppliers and not being offered credit in the future.

- **Working Capital Cycle =**
Inventory days + Receivables days – Payables days.

- **Asset turnover (non-current assets) =**

$$\frac{\text{Revenue}}{\text{non-current assets}}$$

Financial position

- **Interest cover =**

$$\frac{\text{Profit from operations}}{\text{Finance costs}}$$

- This shows how many times the interest charge can be paid out of the current profits. It is a measure of security - the higher the ratio, the more secure the interest payment.

- **Gearing =**

$$\frac{\text{Non-current liabilities}}{\text{Total equity + Non-current liabilities}}$$

- This ratio shows the proportion of debt to total finance in the business (equity plus debt). The higher the gearing ratio, the riskier a company is seen to be as debt interest must be paid out before dividends.

Limitations of ratio analysis

- Ratios do not provide answers; they merely highlight significant features or trends in the financial statements. They usually highlight areas that need further investigation.

- Be mindful of seasonal trade as accounting year-ends are often just after the seasonal trend is over when the business is at its best.

- Watch out for window dressing in the financial statements such as collecting receivables just before the year-end in order to show a larger cash balance and lower receivables than is normal.

- Accounting ratios are based on accounting information and are only as accurate as that underlying accounting information.

- If comparisons are to be made they must be with companies with a similar trade, otherwise the pattern of ratios will be different and the comparisons meaningless.

chapter

10

Recap of key aspects of Management Accounting: Budgeting

- Behavioural aspects of budgeting.
- Basic methods of budgeting.
- Flexed budgets.
- Flexible budgets.
- Materials variances.
- Labour variances.
- Interdependence of variances.
- Variance investigation.
- Reasons for variances.
- Performance indicators.

Behavioural aspects of budgeting

Target setting and motivation

Targets will assist motivation and appraisal if they are at the right level.

- Too hard and people give up.
- Too easy and people won't try hard enough.

An ideal target should be slightly above the anticipated performance level.

Targets should be:

- Communicated in advance.
- Dependent on factors controllable by the individual.
- Based on quantifiable factors.
- Linked to appropriate rewards and penalties.
- Chosen carefully to ensure goal congruence.
- Challenging but achievable.

Participation is generally agreed to help.

Participation

Top-down budgeting (non-participative)

A budget which is set without allowing the ultimate budget holder to have the opportunity to participate in the budgeting process.

Bottom-up budgeting (participative)

A system of budgeting in which budget holders have the opportunity to participate in setting their own budgets.

Advantages of participative budgets	Disadvantages of participative budgets
1. Increased motivation.	1. Senior managers may resent loss of control.
2. Should contain better information, especially in a fast-moving or diverse business.	2. Bad decisions from inexperienced managers.
3. Increases managers' understanding and commitment.	3. Budgets may not be in line with corporate objectives.
4. Better communication.	4. Budget preparation is slower and disputes can arise.
5. Senior managers can concentrate on strategy.	5. Figures may be subject to bias if junior managers either try to impress or set easily achievable targets (budgetary slack).
	6. Certain environments may preclude participation, e.g. sales manager may be faced with long-term contracts already agreed.

Basic methods of budgeting

Incremental (historic)	Zero-based budgeting	Priority-based budgeting	Activity-based budgeting
Starts with previous period's budget or actual results and adds (or subtracts) an incremental amount to cover inflation and other known changes.	Requires cost element to be specifically justified, as though the activities to which the budget relates were being undertaken for the first time.	A competitively ranked listing of high to low priority discrete bids for "decision packages." • All activities are re-evaluated each time a budget is set. • Does not require a zero assumption.	Preparing budgets using overhead costs from activity based costing methodology.
Suitable for stable businesses, where costs are not expected to change significantly.	Without approval, the budget allowance is zero.		
There should be good cost control and limited discretionary costs.	Suitable for allocating resources in areas were spend is discretionary.		

Flexed budgets

For variances to be meaningful and appropriate for use as decision-making tools, a **flexed budget** should be prepared to take into account the change between the budgeted levels of activity (sales and production) and the actual levels.

	Budget	**Flexed budget**	**Actual**
Sales volume	100 units	90 units	90 units
Sales value	£1,000	£900	£990
Variable costs	£500	£450	£495
Fixed costs	£200	£200	£210
Profit	£300	£250	£285

Flexible budgets

A **fixed** budget contains information on costs and revenue for one level of activity. A **flexible** budget shows the same information, but for a number of different levels of activity.

	Low	Normal	High
Activity level	80,000 units	100,000 units	120,000 units
Revenue	£3,200,000	£4,000,000	£4,800,000
Variable costs	£1,440,000	£1,800,000	£2,160,000
Fixed costs	£300,000	£300,000	£300,000
Profit	£1,460,000	£1,900,000	£2,340,000

A **flexible** budget model makes it possible to quickly amend the line items in the event of some unforeseen complication. For example, should sales volume suddenly drop, affecting the amount of generated revenue, the flexible format makes it easy to quickly change the amounts associated with specific line items to reflect the new set of circumstances.

The ability to quickly adjust a flexible budget to take into account changes in output levels or shifts in income means that a business can move quickly to meet the new circumstances. By contrast, a fixed budget, that is based on a single set of projections and allows no room for adjustments without going through a complicated approval process, wastes valuable time and money that could be used more efficiently.

Materials variances

1   Materials price variance

The material price variance is calculated compared to what we expected to pay, so that we can work out whether we have paid too much or too little for our materials.

We always use the **Purchased quantity** in the calculation and we compare the Actual price paid and the **Standard** (expected) price.

Formula:	
Actual quantity purchased × Actual price V Actual quantity purchased × Standard price	
Materials price variance	£X F/ A

We can also use what we call the Did and Should method to work out an answer.

x units did cost	£X
x units should have cost @ £x	£X
Variance	£X F/A

2 Materials Usage variance

The materials usage variance is calculated so that we can work out whether we have used too much or too little material to manufacture our goods in the period.

We always use the Used quantity of material in the calculation, and we compare the Actual amount of materials used with the Standard (expected) amount of materials that we should use to make the actual volume of goods in the period (the activity level).

Formula:	
Actual quantity used × Standard price V Standard quantity used for actual production × Standard price	
Materials usage variance	£X F/A

We can also use what we call the Did and Should method to work out an answer.

x units did use	x	kgs
x units should have used @ 2 sq metres per box	x	kgs
	x	kgs
Multiplied by the standard (expected) price	*£x	
So variance is	£X	

Labour variances

1 Labour rate variance

The labour rate variance is calculated so that we can work out whether or not we have paid the correct hourly rate to the direct labour employees. We always use the total hours paid and we compare the Actual hourly rate paid and the standard (expected) hourly rate.

Formula:	
Actual labour hours paid × Actual rate	
V	
Actual labour hours paid × Standard rate	
Labour rate variance	£X F/A

When calculating the labour rate variance we could again use what we call the Did and Should method to work out the answer.

x hours did cost	£X
x hours should have cost @ £X per hour	£X
	___
Variance	£X

2   Labour efficiency variance

The labour efficiency variance is calculated so that we can work out whether we have used too much or too little labour to manufacture our goods in the period.

We always use the worked quantity of hours and we compare the actual number of hours worked and the standard (expected) number of hours that we should work to make the volume of goods in the period (the activity level).

Formula:

Actual hours worked × Standard rate

V

Standard hours worked for actual production × Standard rate

Labour efficiency variance   £X F/A

We can use the Did and Should method to calculate the labour efficiency also.

X units did use	X hours
X units should have used @ x minutes per box	X hours
	―――――
	X hours
Multiplied by the standard (expected) rate	× £X per hour
so variance is	£X

3 Idle time variance

The idle time variance is calculated as the difference between the direct labour hours paid and the direct labour hours worked. It is a balancing figure and it is always adverse. It is always calculated using the standard (expected) hourly rate.

> Actual hours paid × Standard rate
> V
> Actual hours worked × Standard rate

Hours paid for	X hours
Hours worked	X hours
	X hours
Multiplied by the standard (expected) rate	× £X per hour
so variance is	£X F / A

Interdependence of variances

The cause of a variance may affect another variance in a corresponding or opposite way.

For example, workers trying to improve productivity (favourable labour efficiency variance) might become careless and waste more material (adverse material usage variance).

Variance investigation

Variance calculations are just the starting point. Next, management need to decide which variances are worth investigating. To do this they will consider the following.

- How big is the variance?
  - Absolute size
  - Relative size as a % of standard
  - Overall trend.
- Is it favourable or adverse?
- Possible reasons for it
  - Planning errors
  - Measurement problems
  - Random factors
  - Operational issues.
- Controllability.
- Cost v benefit of investigation.

- Likelihood of a problem, based on past experience.
- The overall picture given by all the variances.

Management will seek to assign responsibility for the variances so they can be investigated further.

Reasons for variances

Variance		Possible causes
Materials:	Price	Bulk discounts
		Different suppliers/ Different materials
		Unexpected delivery costs
		Different buying procedures
	Usage	Different quality material
		Theft, obsolescence, deterioration
		Different quality of staff
		Different mix of material
		Different batch sizes and trim loss
Labour:	Rate	Different class of labour
		Excessive overtime
		Productivity bonuses
		National wage negotiations
		Union action

Variance		Possible causes
	Efficiency	Different levels of skill
		Different working conditions
		The learning effect
		Lack of supervision
		Works to rule
		Machine breakdowns
		Lack of material
		Lack of orders
		Strikes (if paid)
		Too long over coffee breaks
Overhead:	Price	Change in nature of overhead
		Unforeseen price changes
	Volume	Excessive idle time
		Increase in workforce

Performance indicators

The examiner has grouped these measures into four areas:

1 **Quality** indicators such as reject rates.

2 **Efficiency indicators,** such as the number of products made per labour hour, or idle time ratios.

3 **Capacity measures,** such as machine utilisation ratios (or 'asset utilisation' ratios).

4 **Simple financial measures** such as the average selling price, profit percentage of sales revenue, material cost of material per unit of purchase, labour rate per hour, cost per unit of production and sales and cost variances.

11

Recap of key aspects of Management Accounting: Decision and control

- Differences between absorption and marginal costing.
- MC and TAC – Summary.
- Relevant costing.
- Breakeven analysis.
- Limiting factors.
- Standard costing.
- Variance analysis – overview.
- Materials variances.
- Labour variances.
- Variable overhead variances.

- Fixed overhead variances.
- Variance investigation.
- Performance measurement.
- Profitability ratios.
- Liquidity ratios.
- Working capital ratios.
- Investor ratio.
- The balanced scorecard.
- Lifecycle costing.
- Target costing.
- Activity Based Costing (ABC).

Differences between absorption and marginal costing

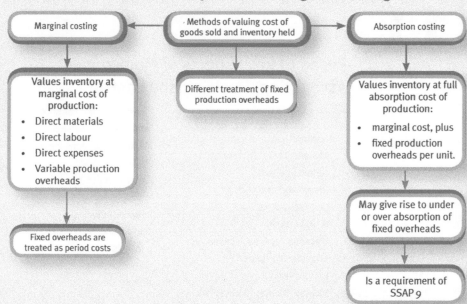

MC and TAC – summary

Marginal costing (MC)

In marginal costing, units of inventory are valued incorporating only variable production costs.

- More consistent with short term decision making techniques as most focus on contribution.
- Can also be simpler as fixed costs do not have to be apportioned.
- Cannot boost profit simply by making more units (unlike TAC).

Total absorption costing

In absorption costing, inventories are valued by incorporating all production costs, both fixed and variable.

- Suitable for financial reporting.
- Suitable for 'full cost plus' pricing, ensuring that all costs are covered.

- Profit fluctuates less when faced with seasonal trade.

Overhead absorption is achieved by means of a predetermined Overhead Absorption Rate (OAR).

Relevant costing

Relevant cash flows are future incremental cash flows which arise as a result of a decision being taken

The relevant cash flow is therefore the difference between:

A. the cash flow which arises if the course of action is taken

B. the cash flow which arises if it is not.

Ignore:
- Sunk costs.
- Committed costs.
- Non-cash items.
- Book values.
- Apportioned costs.

Breakeven analysis

Breakeven point

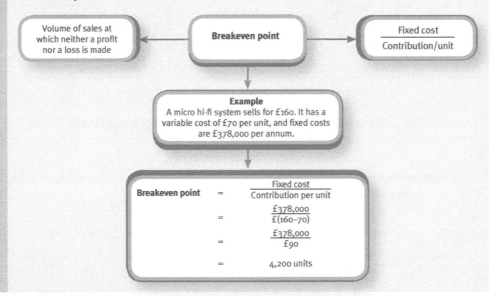

Volume of sales at which neither a profit nor a loss is made

Breakeven point

$$\frac{\text{Fixed cost}}{\text{Contribution/unit}}$$

Example

A micro hi-fi system sells for £160. It has a variable cost of £70 per unit, and fixed costs are £378,000 per annum.

Breakeven point	=	$\dfrac{\text{Fixed cost}}{\text{Contribution per unit}}$
	=	$\dfrac{£378,000}{£(160-70)}$
	=	$\dfrac{£378,000}{£90}$
	=	4,200 units

Margin of safety

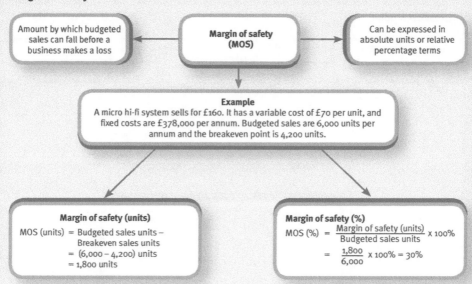

Amount by which budgeted sales can fall before a business makes a loss

Margin of safety (MOS)

Can be expressed in absolute units or relative percentage terms

Example

A micro hi-fi system sells for £160. It has a variable cost of £70 per unit, and fixed costs are £378,000 per annum. Budgeted sales are 6,000 units per annum and the breakeven point is 4,200 units.

Margin of safety (units)

MOS (units) = Budgeted sales units – Breakeven sales units
= (6,000 – 4,200) units
= 1,800 units

Margin of safety (%)

$$\text{MOS (\%)} = \frac{\text{Margin of safety (units)}}{\text{Budgeted sales units}} \times 100\%$$

$$= \frac{1,800}{6,000} \times 100\% = 30\%$$

Target profit

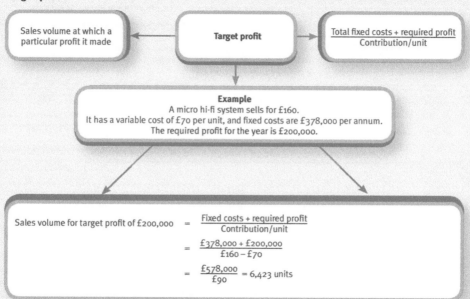

Sales volume at which a particular profit it made

Target profit

$$\frac{\text{Total fixed costs + required profit}}{\text{Contribution/unit}}$$

Example

A micro hi-fi system sells for £160.
It has a variable cost of £70 per unit, and fixed costs are £378,000 per annum.
The required profit for the year is £200,000.

Sales volume for target profit of £200,000 $= \dfrac{\text{Fixed costs + required profit}}{\text{Contribution/unit}}$

$= \dfrac{£378,000 + £200,000}{£160 - £70}$

$= \dfrac{£578,000}{£90} = 6,423 \text{ units}$

Limiting factors

Definition

Key factor analysis is a technique used when we have one resource that is in scarce supply and we can make more than one type of product using that resource. Key factor analysis determines how to use this resource in such a way that profits are maximised.

Approach to key factor analysis

↓

(1) Determine the limiting factor or key factor that is in scarce supply

↓

(2) Calculate the contribution per unit generated by each product

↓

$$\frac{\text{Contribution per unit}}{\text{Number of units of scarce resource needed}}$$

← (3) Calculate the contribution per unit of scarce resource for each product

↓

(4) Select the product with the highest contribution per unit of scarce resource and make this first

Standard costing

Objective is to control the business:

1. Set up standard costs, prepare budgets and set targets.

2. Measure actual performance.

3. Compare actual v budget via variances.

4. Investigate reasons for differences and take action.

Types of standard:

- Ideal standards are based on optimal operating conditions with maximum efficiency and are usually unobtainable under normal conditions.

- Attainable standards are based on existing operating conditions.

- Basic standards are left unchanged from one period to another.

- Current standards are adjusted for each period.

Standard cost card

The standard cost card is a schedule that gives the standard costs that a unit of a product **should** incur.

Example	
	£
Materials (2kg at £3 per kg)	6
Labour (0.5 hours at £18 per hour)	9
Overheads (0.5 hours at £20 per hour)	10
Total standard cost per unit	25

Advantages of standard costing

- Comparison of actual costs to standard enables management to judge performance.

- Facilitates 'management by exception' – i.e. concentrate on investigating the most significant variances.

- Simplifies bookkeeping if Inventories are valued at standard.

Disadvantages of standard costing

- Standards can quickly become out of date.

- Establishing standards, monitoring of system and investigation of variances is costly.

- Unrealistic standards can demotivate staff.

Variance analysis – overview

Comparing like with like

When calculating variances it is vital that you compare like with like.

For each cost we compare the actual cost with how much it **should** have cost to produce the same actual level of output:

Actual cost

$\updownarrow$ Variance

Standard cost of
actual production

Materials variances

Materials Price variance

This is based on the actual quantity of materials purchased:

Materials purchased did cost

Actual quantity purchased $\times$ Actual price $= X$

Materials purchased should have cost

Actual quantity purchased $\times$ Standard price $= X$

} Price variance

Materials Usage variance

Quantity actually used at SP

Actual quantity used $\times$ Standard price $= X$

Quantity that should have been used at SP

Standard quantity used* $\times$ Standard price $= X$

} Usage variance

* i.e. quantity that should have been used to make actual output.

Reasons for variances

Price Variance

1. Wrong standards.

2. Lower/higher quality material.

3. Different supplier.

4. Good/poor purchasing.

5. External factors (inflation, exchange rates etc).

Usage Variance

1. Wrong standards.

2. Lower/higher quality of material.

3. Lower/higher quality of labour.

4. Theft.

Labour variances

Labour Rate variance

Hours paid did cost

Actual hours	x	Actual rate	=	X	}

Hours paid should have cost

Actual hours	x	Standard rate	=	X	} Rate variance

Labour Efficiency variance

Hours actually paid at SR

Actual hours	x	Standard rate	=	X	}

Hours that should have been paid at SR

Standard hours*	x	Standard rate	=	X	} Efficiency variance

* i.e. hours firm should have worked to make the actual output

Reasons for variances

Rate Variance

1. Wrong standards.
2. Wage inflation.
3. Lower/higher skilled employees.
4. Unplanned overtime or bonuses.

Efficiency variance

1. Wrong standards.
2. Lower/higher morale.
3. Lower/higher skilled employees.
4. Lower/higher quality of material.

Variable overhead variances

Variable overhead expenditure variance

Hours worked did cost

Actual hours worked   x   Actual rate   = X

Hours worked should have cost

Actual hours worked   x   Standard rate = X

} Expenditure variance

Variable overhead efficiency variance

Hours actually worked at SR

Actual hours worked   x   Standard rate = X

Hours that should have been worked at SR

Standard hours*   x   Standard rate = X

} Efficiency variance

* i.e. hours firm should have worked to make the actual output

Reasons for variances

Expenditure Variance

1. Wrong standards.
2. Rate inflation.

Efficiency variance

1. Wrong standards.
2. Lower/higher morale.
3. Lower/higher skilled employees.
4. Lower/higher quality of material.

Fixed overhead variances

Definition

The total fixed overhead variance is the difference between the actual fixed overhead, and the absorbed fixed overhead.

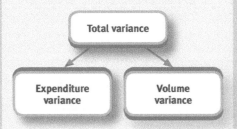

Fixed overhead expenditure variance (MC and TAC)

$$\left.\begin{array}{ll} \text{Actual fixed overheads} & = X \\ \text{Budgeted fixed overheads} & = X \end{array}\right\} \begin{array}{l}\text{Expenditure variance}\end{array}$$

Note: this is the original budget unadjusted for differences in output.

Fixed overhead volume variance (TAC only)

The volume variance is the difference between the budgeted overhead absorbed and the actual overhead absorbed.

$$\left.\begin{array}{lll} \text{Budgeted production} & \times & \dfrac{\text{Standard cost}}{\text{per unit}} = X \\ \text{Actual production} & \times & \dfrac{\text{Standard cost}}{\text{per unit}} = X \end{array}\right\} \begin{array}{l}\text{Volume var.}\end{array}$$

Reasons for fixed overhead variances

Fixed Overhead Expenditure Variance (MC and TAC)

The expenditure variance is the simplest fixed overhead variance and simply compares the original budgeted figure with actual. The variance will be due to poor budgeting or to a price rise.

e.g. rent increased by landlord.

Fixed Overhead Volume Variance (TAC)

The volume variance is due to the volume of production changing. A favourable (adverse) variance reflects the fact that more (less) units were made than planned. This could be due to:

- Poor budgeting.
- Labour efficiency.
- Availability of resources (e.g. shortage of materials).

Variance investigation

Variance calculations are just the starting point. Next, management need to decide which variances are worth investigating. To do this they will consider the following.

- How big is the variance?
  - Absolute size.
  - Relative size as a % of standard.
  - Overall trend.
- Is it favourable or adverse?
- Possible reasons for it.
  - Planning errors.
  - Measurement problems.
  - Random factors.
  - Operational issues.
- Controllability.
- Cost v benefit of investigation.
- Likelihood of a problem, based on past experience.

- The overall picture given by all the variances.

Management will seek to assign responsibility for the variances so they can be investigated further.

CBA focus

Performance appraisal is a very important topic. Two styles of task are commonplace:

Some tasks ask you to assess the organisation using ratios and other KPIs.

Some tasks give some new circumstances and require you to produce forecasts/revised ratios based on those changes.

Try to relate your comments to any details given in the scenario:

e.g. a switch to more expensive materials could explain changes in margins and quality.

Try to discuss both financial and non-financial indicators.

Performance measurement

An effective system of performance measurement is critical if the business is to be controlled.

Performance indicators can be:

- quantitative (i.e. expressed in numbers); or

- qualitative (i.e. not expressed in numbers). For example, satisfied/not satisfied or grade poor to excellent.

The 3Es

- **Economy** is the degree to which low prices were paid for the inputs of the business.

- **Effectiveness** is the degree to which the business objectives have been met.

- **Efficiency** is the relationship between inputs and outputs achieved, i.e. that as few inputs as possible have been used to achieve a particular output level of the desired quality.

Benchmarking

Need a suitable basis for comparison.

- Internal benchmarking. For example, by division.
- Competitive benchmarking.
- Activity (or process) benchmarking.
- Generic benchmarking – look at conceptually similar processes.

Profitability ratios

Return on capital employed (ROCE)

Capital employed is normally measured as non-current assets plus current assets less current liabilities and represents the long–term investment in the business. It is also measured as owners' capital plus long–term liabilities. Return on capital employed is frequently regarded as the best measure of profitability.

$$ROCE = \frac{\text{Profit before interest and taxation (PBIT)}}{\text{Capital employed}} \times 100\%$$

Note that the profit before interest is used, because the loan capital rewarded by that interest is included in capital employed.

A low return on capital employed (assets used) is caused by either a low profit margin or a low asset turnover or both. This can be seen by breaking down the primary ROCE ratio into its two components: profit margin and asset turnover.

$$ROCE = \frac{PBIT}{Capital\ employed}$$
$$= \frac{PBIT}{Revenue} \times \frac{Revenue}{Capital\ employed}$$
$$= Profit\ margin \times Asset\ turnover$$

Profit margin (on revenue)

$$Profit\ margin = \frac{Profit\ before\ interest\ and\ taxation}{Revenue} \times 100\%$$

A low margin indicates low selling prices or high costs or both.

Asset turnover

This will show the extent to which a company is utilising its assets to generate turnover:

$$Asset\ turnover = \frac{Revenue}{Capital\ employed}$$

A low turnover shows that a company is not generating a sufficient volume of business for the size of the asset base. This may be remedied by increasing sales or by disposing of some of the assets or both.

Gross profit margin

$$Gross\ profit\ margin = \frac{Gross\ profit}{Revenue} \times 100\%$$

The gross profit margin focuses on the trading account. A low margin could indicate selling prices too low or cost of sales too high.

Liquidity ratios

Current ratio

This indicates the extent to which the claims of short–term payables are covered by assets that are expected to be converted to cash.

$$\text{Current ratio} = \frac{\text{Current assets}}{\text{Current liabilities}}$$

Quick ratio (Acid test ratio)

This is calculated in the same way as the current ratio except that inventories are excluded from current assets, since they may not be converted into cash very quickly.

$$\text{Quick ratio} = \frac{\text{Current assets} - \text{inventory}}{\text{Current liabilities}}$$

This ratio is a much better test of immediate solvency.

Working capital ratios

Receivables collection period (Receivable days)

This is computed by dividing the receivables by the average daily sales to determine the number of days' sales held in receivables.

$$\text{Receivables collection period} = \frac{\text{Trade receivables}}{\text{Credit sales}} \times 365 \text{ days}$$

A long average collection period probably indicates poor credit control. If a company offers standard terms to its credit customers (e.g. 30 days credit), then the actual period of credit taken can be compared to the standard period.

Payables payment period

This is computed by dividing the payables by the average daily credit purchases to determine the number of days purchases held in payables. This tells us how long we are taking to pay our creditors. Too long a payment period may mean that they refuse to sell us goods in the future.

$$\text{Payables payment period} = \frac{\text{Trade payables}}{\text{Credit purchases}} \times 365 \text{ days}$$

Inventory holding period

This ratio indicates whether inventory levels are justified in relation to sales.

$$\text{Inventory holding period} = \frac{\text{Inventory}}{\text{Cost of sales}} \times 365 \text{ days}$$

Investor ratio

Gearing ratio

$$\text{Gearing ratio} = \text{Debt} / \text{Equity} \times 100$$

This ratio measures the proportion of assets invested in the business that are financed by borrowing.

A high gearing ratio means that the business is financed by a lot of debt, which can be dangerous. High levels of interest will be payable which the company may not be able to afford in a year of low profit.

The balanced scorecard

From strategic objectives to performance indicators

Strategic objectives

↓

Chosen strategies

↓

Critical (or key) success factors (CSFs)

↓

Key performance indicators (KPIs)

The balanced scorecard performance management system

	Financial perspective	Customer perspective	Internal business process perspective	Innovation and learning perspective
Strategic objective	Shareholder satisfaction	Customer satisfaction	Manufacturing excellence	New product innovation
CSF	Grow shareholder wealth	Achieve preferred supplier status	State-of-the-art process plant	Successful new product development
KPIs	• ROCE • Growth %	• Number of customer partnerships	• Cycle times • Unit cost • % yield	• % of revenues represented by new products

Lifecycle costing

All products go through lifecycles

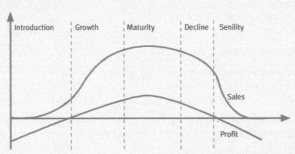

As shown by the difference between the revenue and cost curves, the pattern of costs over the lifecycle does not match that of revenue.

In particular, there will be high development costs during the introduction stage.

Traditional financial accounting has the following problems in this respect:

- It will look at the profit in a particular year, rather than assessing profitability over the whole lifecycle.
- Research costs are often written off in the year in which they are incurred rather than matching against (later) revenue.

Target costing

Many firms operate a 'cost-plus' pricing system, where the selling price of a product is calculated by adding a mark-up to the production cost.

Target costing is the reverse of this process:

1 The firm estimates the likely product price by looking at market conditions, competition, etc.

2 A target mark-up % is deducted from the price to give a target cost.

3 Production then sees if it can produce the product at the cost required.

Example

R plc makes fridges. The current cost per unit is £100 and R sells them for £200, a mark-up of 100%. Due to increased competition, R feels that a selling price of £160 would be more competitive.

Assuming the mark up of 100% is still required, calculate the target cost.

Solution

Target price = £160

Target cost = 160 x 100/200 = £80

The production department needs to try to save £20 per unit on cost.

Activity Based Costing (ABC)

Step 1 Identify major activities.

Step 2 Identify appropriate cost drivers.

Step 3 Collect costs into pools based upon the activities (note: this is usually done for you in a question/task)

Step 4 Charge costs to units of production based on cost driver rate.

$$\text{Cost driver rate} = \frac{\text{Cost pool}}{\text{Level of cost driver}}$$

Examples of cost drivers

- Machine costs could be charged using machine hours.

- Quality control costs could be charged using number of inspections.

- Set-up costs could be charged using number of set-ups.

Benefits and Limitations of ABC

Benefits	Limitations
1. Provides more accurate product line costings.	1. Little evidence to date that ABC improves corporate profitability.
2. Is flexible enough to analyse costs by cost objects other than products, such as processes, areas of managerial responsibility and customers.	2. ABC information is historic and internally orientated and therefore lacks direct relevance for future strategic decisions.
3. Provides meaningful financial (periodic cost driver rates) and non-financial (periodic cost driver volume) measures.	3. Practical problems such as cost driver selection.
4. Aids identification and understanding of cost behaviour and thus has the potential to improve cost estimation.	
5. Provides a more logical, acceptable and comprehensible basis for costing work.	

Index